SPACE COLORING BOOK BELONGS TO

coloring book

MERMAID ON SPACE

BEAR ON SPACE

ANGRY CAT IN SPACE

SPACE GRAVITY WITH CAT

DINOSAUR WITH ALIEN ON SPACE

CAT SLEEP ON SPACE

ASTRONAUT MEET WITH ALIEN

ASTRONAUT CHECKING SOIL ON MARS

ALIEN SHIP

MAN ON MOON

ASTRONAUT WALK ON MARS

CAT COUPLE ON SPACE

COMET

ASTRONAUT CHRISTMAS PARTY

CAT ENJOY SPACE JOURNEY

UNICORN ON SATURN

SPACE PHOTOGRAPHY

CAT LOST GRAVITY

OCTOPUS ON SPACE

CAT ASTRONAUT

SPACECRAFT

MR. FOX ASTRONAUT

SPACE

NAME ALL PLANETS